ANDREW MARTIN

INTERNATIONAL
INTERIOR DESIGN
REVIEW

VOLUME 5

MARTIN WALLER · SARAH STEWART-SMITH

ANDREW MARTIN

INTERNATIONAL

EDITOR: MARTIN WALLER
TEXT: SARAH STEWART-SMITH
PROJECT EXECUTIVE: HANNAH GUTTERIDGE
PRODUCT DESIGN: GRAPHICOM DESIGN

First Published in 2001 by

ANDREW MARTIN
INTERNATIONAL

ISBN 0 9530045 2 X

Reproduction by Yale Press. Printed by Artes Gráficas Toledo S.A.U.
D.L. TO: 712 - 2001

ACKNOWLEDGMENTS

The author and publisher wish to thank all the owners and designers of the projects
featured in this book.

They also thank the following photographers:

Sven Everaert, Christian Sarraman, Reto Guntli, Jessica Fulford-Dobson, Tim Motion, Steve Stephens,
Ralph Scott, Simon Kenny, Luis Azevedo, Iain Kemp, John Gott, Joseph Sy, Richard Waite, Ulso Tsang,
Peter Aprahamian, Jacques Dirand, Lark Smothermon, David Marlow, Girogio Baroni (front cover),
Deyana Ahmadi, Andrew Kennedy, Mark Green, Earl Carter, Jack Sarafian, Francisco Almeida Dias,
Michael Maynard, Barker Evans, Joy Von Tiedmann, Rodrigo Moreno, Paula Wilson, Paul Ratigan,
Victor Albrow, Ales Jungmann, James Morris, Reto Halme (back cover), Anne Manglerud.

INTRODUCTION

The obsession with interior design is not new. Alexander the Great was famously exercised by the look of the great cities he conjured into being. George Washington fretted about the daintiest detail of his house at Mount Vernon even whilst laying the foundations of the United States. When we look back to the great civilizations of antiquity, we are impressed by their politics, their military power and their artistic achievements. But we are most fascinated by how they lived, how their houses looked and we tend to judge their greatness by the luxury of their interiors.

We love to hear about luxurious fabrics travelling the silk road, tiles transported from the Levant, the gilding in Byzantium and the treasures of the Nile. It was the merchants that drove these cities to greatness and it is as true today as it ever was. Cities that have been broken by tragedy such as in old Yugoslavia, aspire to return to the leisure, wealth and sensibilities where interior design is high on the priorities. It's a sign of peace and prosperity and an indication of the golden age in which we live. Enjoy it while we can.

This volume brings together the best interior designers from each corner of the world. From the sophistication of Washington DC to the casual charm of Norway, the hitech of Hong Kong to the grandeur of France. It demonstrates that the world hasn't shrunk to an homogeneous identity. The romance of diversity is still with us. Only the interest is universal.

MARTIN WALLER

Jean de Meulder

Designer: Jean de Meulder. **Company:** Jean de Meulder, Antwerp, Belgium. **Work:** Mainly residential projects, plus a yacht and seaside shoe shop. **Signature:** Simplicity, functionality, authenticity and timelessness... and I always mix my own colours. **Colour:** Whenever I prepare a colour, it is generally a composition of three different colours to create an off tone. These are not secondary colours, I call them tertiary colours and they bring the most serenity to a space. Each time I mix a colour, I try to put some grey into it to give it a silvery shine. That softens the strict lines of the architecture. I like to use many colours that are close to one another instead of using contrasting colours. That is why I use very off greens that look almost grey like lavender green and celadon green. **Best idea:** Doing this job. **Big break:** There have been three: the first was being responsible for the design of all the Pan American ticket offices in Europe; then living in Rome for three years; and finally in the late seventies, realising that there was a need for an interior architect in Paris at a time when the idea of mixing old and new was brand new. **Biggest influence:**

'The general harmony of a house should be one of openness and calm.'

Modern art. Not just because I am personally interested, but, because most of my clients have good collections and I have to design for and around the art. **Motivation:** Passion. I do this with as much pleasure now as when I began working. **New directions:** Interiors are becoming softer in a more comfortable way, in both atmosphere and furnishings - we all need more calm because of the stress and business of modern life. **Favourite painting:** An important and striking piece in salt, burnt wood and lead, by Pierre Paolo Calzolari. It is a three-dimensional abstract composition. **Favourite movie star:** Juliette Binoche. She is so sweet and so strong, and handsome, sexy and extremely intelligent. **Favourite country:** Italy. There is the beautiful scenery in Tuscany;

the hills covered with Cyprus and olive trees... the outstanding talent of designers in Milan... the furniture, car industry, marvellous wines and great cuisine. But above all, I love the standing breakfasts in the small corner shops. **Free time:** Listening to music and modern art. **Top shop:** Colette in Paris. It is like a department store but does not look like a department store. There are objects, books, clothes, everything, and it is all of the highest quality. There is even a water bar where you can drink 50 or so different waters from all over the world. **Pet hates:** Fashionable colours because they are not timeless, fake materials like faux fur and Formica and I also hate coordinated fabrics, thick-piled rugs and undersized furniture.

'I prefer to use a combination of many different colours that are very close to one another.'

La Luna Restaurant, Antwerp.

MM Design

Designer: Monika Apponyi. **Company:** MM Design, London. **Work:** Mostly residential, the bulk of which is on the Continent, with commercial jobs such as a golf club in Germany. **Signature:** Classic in the real classic sense... my work is warm, welcoming and not at all stark. **Colour:** There is a place for every colour and I am not against using any colour as long as it does not jar. What interests me is the distribution of colour - colours can be wild and fashionable as long as they are not over-powering. **Best idea:** Having Nora Bentink, who does nothing but source things... sheets, antiques, objects, china and paintings... it makes the clients very happy. **Big break:** Doing two room sets - one in 1990 and the other in 1991. One was a grand silk and velvet red room and the other a blue and white bedroom. Each time I won the public vote. **Biggest influence:** Comfort and some sense of order... and the American interior designer, Billy Baldwin whose work in the fifties and sixties was modern, chic and timeless. **Motivation:** The people I deal with and getting the job right. **New directions:** To simplify things where possible so that you have a tailored but less grand feeling, and using more technology to make life easier. **Favourite painting:** The 16th century painting The Girl with the Pearl Earring (Vermeer). It is just beautiful. The face, the texture and the colours are out of this world. **Favourite movie star:** Lauren Bacall - she is a woman of substance. **Favourite country:** Greece - the Greek islands. Each island is completely different to the next and they have simplicity and sheer beauty. **Free time:** Travel, see friends and being with my children. **Top shop:** For clothes it has to be Armani... but I am not a big shopper... **Pet hates:** Over-the-top ornate kitchens, over-the-top people who are not true to themselves and I hate homes that are not loved or looked after.

'People want less colour, so the only way to introduce excitement is in the various textures and differences in touch.'

'I could not live with bare
tables, one lily in a vase
and one newspaper on the
coffee table and nor could
any of my clients.'

Czarska Limited

First Class

Designer: Isobel Czarska. **Company:** Czarska Limited, London. **Work:** A specialisation in aviation projects such as The Golden Lounge at Terminal 3, Heathrow, plus commercial residential projects and swimming pools. **Signature:** Sensual, comfortable, simple spaces - everything I do is very plain with the focus on shape and form. **Colour:** Because we live in the northern hemisphere and light is so precious, I like everything to be very blond and natural. It helps maximise on natural light. **Best idea:** The expansion joints for The Golden Lounge at Terminal 3, Heathrow. When you add a structure to an existing building you have to allow for three-way movement. Generally this joint can make a mess of finishes, but we developed a way of going from a soft surface to a hard surface by having a very slight, rubberised trim that you would hardly notice. **Big break:** Over a decade ago,

I won the Cathay Pacific contract to develop the First Class brand for both cabins and the lounges in Western Europe. **Biggest influence:** Growing up in Africa and travelling with my parents... and then later travelling in Japan. The Japanese are truly artistic and I love the aesthetic. **Motivation:** The challenge of solving specific problems combined with the dynamic of the creative process. You think of an idea, germinate it and then make it grow. I am also fascinated by the huge effects we can have on peoples' businesses. **New directions:** Branching out into hotel design. **Favourite**

painting: Leonardo da Vinci's Portrait of a Lady with an Ermine (1485). It's got this unbelievable translucence and extraordinary power that gives the painting a glow from within. It is amazing. **Favourite movie star:** Pierce Brosnan for that whole Cary Grant sort of thing... and Sean Connery is always divine. **Favourite country:** Italy... for the way of life, sensuality and the architecture. **Free time:** What free time? But I am a serious collector of British studio pottery. **Top shop:** Armani. I am an Armani person. **Pet hates:** Thoughtlessness and lack of due care and attention.

'Everything I do is very plain with the focus on shape and form. Then the sensual elements - light, texture, natural materials and water - create the comfort.'

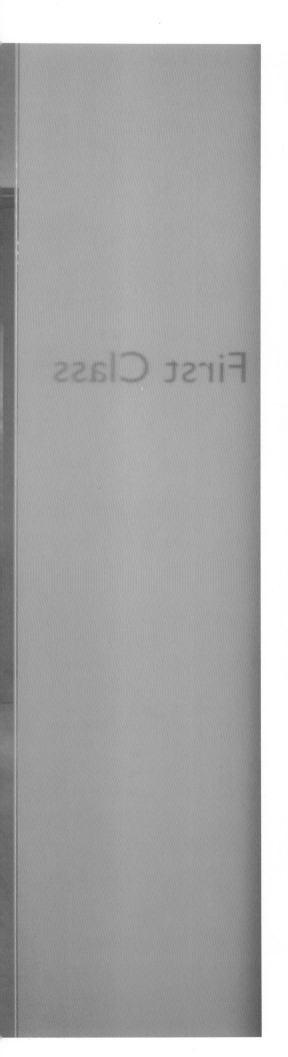

First Class

Malaysia Airlines, Heathrow Terminal 3.

Hennie Interiors

Designer: Helene Forbes Hennie. **Company:** Hennie Interiors, Oslo, Norway. **Work:** Primarily residential work and restaurant projects. **Signature:** Having both a contemporary and a very high tech approach to solving the puzzle of how to create the best interior. The solution has to work for the client and with the building. **Colour:** This year has been about non-coloured interiors because everybody wants a peaceful environment. That has meant we have been using many earthy and neutral combinations, but I like to use colour, as it is very inspirational. Colour can persuade you to eat, persuade you to sleep and so on... just as for some people red is very relaxing, to others it implies danger. To feel relaxed, I would want to sit in a blue, lilac or cream room. **Best idea:** Working as a team within a small company. It is not just about me, it is the combination of us all that makes it work. **Big break:** Working with a real estate company. It has taught us a great deal, particularly that interiors must be practical.

Biggest influence: The people around me, and of course, the client. **Motivation:** Having a good relationship with the client. When it is fun, the work and result is always better. **New directions:** Creating homes that are much more comfortable so that the space does not look or feel hard and cold in any way. **Favourite painting:** The Mona Lisa is brilliant. It is astonishing, because you see something different in her face each time you look.

Favourite movie star: Jodie Foster. She is both charismatic and a perfectionist. **Favourite country:** Spain. I have lived there and visit often because there are so many wonderful places that are not tourist haunts. **Free time:** Being with my husband, children and friends. **Top shop:** The Conran Shop in London... I like things that have to do with my work. **Pet hates:** Bad lighting, especially in restaurants and lack of order or harmony.

'We tend to begin with lighting because that creates atmosphere.'

'Colour can persuade you to eat, it can persuade you to sleep... red can be very relaxing for some, while to others it can signal danger or vitality.'

Ciao Ellie and Clare Designs

Designers: Clare Hazell and Ellie Phelan. **Company:** Ciao, Ellie and Clare Designs, London. **Work:** Both residential and commercial projects that have included a home on the coast of Africa and an office for a television company. **Signature:** Huge Comfort. And we try to manipulate the senses - touch, sight, sound and scent - to create an all round environment. **Colour:** The location and house tell us what colour to use, but we tend toward neutrals and warm them up with oysters and various beige tones. These are then highlighted with cherry. I am absolutely mad about a blackish cherry red and the colour black. **Best idea:** Using spaces for many purposes. It is such a great discipline and I try to make each space as multi-purpose as possible. **Big break:** Forming this partnership to create Ciao. **Biggest influence:** Colour... and travel. **Motivation:** Finding a way of getting the maximum out of a building; how to make it more usable and economical. **New directions:** Making minimal more comfortable and adding more colour like

aqua and camel and scarlet and ice blue - that last combination is an absolute dead favourite. **Favourite painting:** The Painted Gallery in the Lascaux in Cannes, France, as it is one of the finest examples of Palaeolithic art in the world. **Favourite movie star:** Kermit the Frog (Clare wants to marry him), Jude Law (utterly gorgeous), Cary Grant (for his screwball comedies, his chic and elegance) and Steve McQueen (a real dude). **Favourite country:** Italy... and my favourite place in the world is Rome. The architecture is unbelievable and even the roofs are chic. Clare loves India for

both the colour and the atmosphere. **Free time:** I shuttle between two children and work with the NSPCC and Clare rides and works with The International League for the Protection of Horses. **Top shop:** Hermes. The design is strong and the colours are great and we want to own everything. It is the same with Valentino. **Pet hates:** We loathe cold floors and a cold environment, hate walking into a room that seems identical to one you have seen at least 25 times before and we are not at all keen on salmon pink, apricot, oatmeal or peach tones.

'We use natural dyed Indian silks, because they are so strong and almost edible.'

'We are mad about cherry and black or orange and shocking pink.'

Designer: Shiuli Johanna Davis. **Company:** Shiuli Johanna Interiors, Britain. **Work:** Mainly residential work in Britain and Asia. **Signature:** It has been called Minimal Orientalism, but I like to think of it as a mix of Western contemporary with Oriental simplicity. **Colour:** I don't think I have ever used a colour like scarlet or turquoise... I tend to use a backdrop of whites with stone, ecru, and pistachio, used with warm, earthy colours and a range of browns like mud and silt and grey. My shots of colour would probably be terracotta or ochre. **Best idea:** Getting into this business. I started from scratch eight years ago having been the head of a company that organised conferences. **Big break:** The first was becoming my own client when I moved house and as a result, I learned how difficult it is to be a client, and the second was taking on a client who wanted their entire house done up on a tiny budget. I did it to prove it could be done, knowing that if you can be creative on very little money, you can only be even more

Shiuli Johanna Interiors

creative with a good budget. **Biggest influence:** Wanting to be my own boss working within my own arena. **Motivation:** Passion for this subject. **New directions:** Making Orientalism more comfortable. **Favourite painting:** White Dark III (1995) by Anish Kapoor. His work conveys the idea that a space can be more empty than ever imaginable. **Favourite movie star:** Ralph Fiennes has a mysterious quality and is a superb actor and Audrey Hepburn epitomises elegance and grace. **Favourite country:** India. I am biased because I spent my childhood there but I also love Italy. The food, architecture and people are wonderful in both countries. **Free time:** Dreaming up interiors, going for walks and being with my family. **Top shop:** Takashimaya in New York, for its eclectic mix of interiors and fashion, but there is also a little-known shop called Livingstone Studio in Hampstead in London, where you find interior artefacts mixed with clothes from India and Japan. **Pet hates:** Clutter, unsympathetic lighting, and contrived, glitzy interiors.

'Interiors should push the boundaries and not follow trends.'

'By all means borrow ideas from the past, strip them down to the strongest element and then redevelop the concept.'

Jean-Pierre Heurteau Design

Designer: Jean-Pierre Heurteau. **Company:** Jean-Pierre Heurteau Design, Victoria, Australia. **Work:** Owning and running a design shop and working on both residential and commercial projects. **Signature:** A rich, eclectic look with a European flavour. I am known for animal prints, a lot of gold and strong colour. **Colour:** I cannot live with beige alone and I tend toward colours that don't date like raspberry, red and soft greens - these colours go back centuries. **Best idea:** I did a very OTT but chic all-purple room for an exhibition space in 1990 during the recession. I did it to cheer everyone up. The canopied bed was purple, the wallpaper was purple and the carpet was purple... it put me in another

league. **Big break:** The purple room helped, but the recession was a catalyst because I had to work harder to catch the eye of potential clients. It was a matter of having the courage to stand out. **Biggest influence:** Architectural Digest and The World of Interiors. Between the ages of 18 and 20, when I could not afford to buy these magazines, I used to borrow them from a friend and read them all night long. **Motivation:** The challenge and combination of importing for a shop and working with my clients. **New directions:** Fashion has always driven my interior design and given me a sense of direction. **Favourite painting:** A Landscape of Lorne, by an Australian artist called Buck Master. When I

was younger I always admired his work and I finally acquired this one. It is very serene. **Favourite movie star:** Russell Crowe in Gladiator - it is great to see an Australian doing that calibre of work in Hollywood. **Favourite country:** France... for the food, the people and the stylishness. **Free time:** Looking for things. **Top shop:** Gucci. I have become a maniac for the branch opposite Harvey Nichols in London. The whole experience of the guards with walkie-talkies, the shop, the clothes and the fantasy is wonderful. **Pet hates:** Cheap design... cheap construction, cheap fabrics... and cheap anything with an expensive price tag. And I hate anything dirty. I like things to sparkle.

'I am often inspired by what I see through peoples windows.'

Insight

Designers: Bruce Goers and Anne Kaplan. **Company:** Insight, Illinois, Chicago, USA. **Work:** Mainly residential work with the occasional office in the Chicago area and other places such as Aspen. **Signature:** Creating a somewhat casual look even though it is formal. We like the pretence of a place looking lived-in, something that has a bit of fun and eccentricity. **Colour:** We are not very trendy but we do use colour and like to sneak in more of it than perhaps the client might have originally wanted. If you use enough colour, it comes off as being neutral. It is all in the mix. I have been using lime and a periwinkle, lavender blue, which is warm, but also adds punch and contrast. **Best idea:** Saying 'yes' to this partnership has been my most impulsive and greatest idea. It has given me a tremendous amount of confidence and knowledge, not to mention excitement and challenge. **Big break:** Each and every job as

one progresses to the next. **Biggest influence:** The profession... and remembering to look even in the seediest looking places for inspiration. **Motivation:** The challenge. I love the minute you walk into a finished space and you take in everything before anyone else. **New directions:** We like doing more avant-garde designs when we can inject it into a project. It is important to introduce an edge quality as we are all racing in the 21st century and it does everyone a little bit of good to see something new. **Favourite painting:** The Ways of Worldly Wisdom by the German

painter, Anselm Keifer. It tells the story of his struggle with the recent German past. **Favourite movie star:** I don't have one. **Favourite country:** France for the lifestyle, food and the way the French do their houses and England for, all the excitement in the seasons, for the gardens and the humour. **Free time:** Being with the family, skiing, cooking and just hanging out. **Top shop:** It used to be Chanel, but now it is Oscar de la Renta... but next week it will be something different. **Pet hates:** Anything forced and uncomfortable.

'If you use enough colour it can become almost neutral.'

'We don't want to be so
deadly serious that we
cannot inject a little
surprise.'

'This job takes courage. I don't see it as a science - many of the ideas are bold and I am not always sure that they are going to work. There is always some kind of leap of imagination.'

First Editions

Designer: Geoffrey Lopez and Mark Lonngren. **Company:** First Editions, Woolloomooloo, Australia. **Work:** Both residential and commercial, from penthouses to liquor stores. **Signature:** Variety, never using faux materials and a sense of balance. **Colour:** Textiles set the pace and once we have the fabric, we choose the colour palette. Fashion colours wash over us because the work we do is designed to be there for the long term. **Best idea:** The design and construction of a dining room sideboard. It was for a French art deco inspired apartment, so we used a combination of tooled copper, black marble and fine English sycamore. The application of metal onto sycamore was surprisingly successful. **Big break:** For me it was retraining; the swap from construction to interiors. As a company (we joined up in 1992) the break has been slow and steady, as all our clients have come via word of mouth. **Biggest influence:** People. This business is about people. **Motivation:** Doing the job well... and my partner Karen and my daughter Claudia, who is five years old. **New directions:** A move toward comfort and practicality, but we are not pushing the boundaries. We are looking for longevity and high standards. **Favourite painting:** A thirties watercolour of Dragonrock beach. It is a beautiful soft work, the signature of which is unintelligible. **Favourite movie star:** Bob Hoskins. He is so gritty, real and matter-of-fact. **Favourite country:** Italy for the people, attitudes, general flavour and uniqueness, and Tahiti because it is a paradise in the Pacific. **Free time:** Landscaping and hanging out with Claudia. **Top shop:** Barry's Bizarre in Brookvale, which is north of Sydney. It's a store that is full of junk and stuff, some of which has no obvious worth. I like to find things that have no real value, but because they are interesting, you know you can do something with them. **Pet hates:** Blind acceptance of the current flavour, being ostentatious, heavy, clumsy work, ripping-off clients and general unprofessionalism.

'A room should work for many years until the product is worn out.'

Esboco Interiors

Designer: Nini Andrade Silva. **Company:** Esboco Interiors, Madeira, Portugal. **Work:** Both residential and commercial projects that include hotels, restaurants and bars. **Signature:** I always use white, create simple lines and use warm materials. My friends call me 'Ninimalist'. **Colour:** I love white, because it makes you feel good whether you are happy or not. White is the mother of all colours. **Best idea:** My bedroom. I have the bath behind my bed with a glass screen between the two. The bed is positioned so that I can see the view of the sea. **Big break:** Because I live on an island, everybody knows and trusts me. **Biggest influence:** Peace, light, comfort and the energy in a house. I am becoming more and more of a spiritualist. **Motivation:** The fact that my clients trust me. **New directions:** Becoming more soft and comfortable in my approach to both minimalism and design. **Favourite painting:** Not one, just every one of Picasso's paintings. **Favourite movie star:** I have three. Jack Nicholson is strange, Harrison Ford seems like a simple person and I admire Meryl Streep, because she looks strong. **Favourite country:** Madeira, because it is home. **Free time:** I paint huge canvases, the subject of which is pebbles. My dream is to start a foundation for the poor children living on the streets. **Top shop:** Calvin Klein in New York for both what you can buy and how the shop looks and Donna Karan in London. She is my favourite fashion designer. **Pet hates:** Over-decoration and small objects.

'White is the mother of all colours.'

Disdale Design

Designer: Terence Disdale. **Company:** Disdale Design, London. **Work:** Superyacht design, mixed with some residential work. **Signature:** Having a practical approach and striving for a casual kind of elegance that is timeless. A boat should be practical, just as an apartment must be comfortable. **Colour:** The Mother Nature look on boats has been a great hit - working with limestone rather than marble and leaving timber with a scrubbed finish. Using colours like turquoise and pale coral in conjunction with these materials creates a boat that has a relaxed kind of beach house, conservatory look. In homes, often the possessions, or collection of art will set the pace for colour. In that situation, it is a question of finding a decoration scheme to suit the art. **Best idea:** Solving specific problems to maximise on space or light. In one apartment the windows were set back into a bay and the light in the rooms was quite dingy. We added polished marble to the flooring immediately under the window and then mirrored to each side of the frame. It effectively triples the daylight in the space as it bounces off both mirrored sides and the floor. **Big break:** Designing homes has come from clients who have liked their boats so much that they have asked us to do their houses. With boats it has been a steady process: my first boat was a 45 foot long motor that I designed in 1973 and last year

we launched the largest private yacht in the world, which is 140m long. **Biggest influence:** I am stimulated by everything from fashion to handbags. **Motivation:** Being creative, if I am not working, I paint or draw. **New directions:** Lightening the physical weight of everything possible on a boat, because the heavier it is, the slower it will go... that means using marble that is 5mm thick, glued to honeycomb boards, shaving leather down so it is the thinnest it can possibly be, veneering model makers foam and so on... **Favourite painting:** No one in particular - my favourites are those that have

bits and pieces within them, a mix of 90 percent painting and 10 percent collage. **Favourite movie star:** Steve McQueen was an incredible character. He was very real and a fantastic racing driver. **Favourite country:** South Africa... it's so beautiful. **Free time:** Fishing in India for Mahseer, a huge fresh water fish in India that grow to more than 100 pounds and are very rare. We catch them, give them a kiss and then throw them back into the water. **Top shop:** R. Soles on the King's Road in London. I love cowboy boots. **Pet hates:** Mobile phones in public places... and over varnished wood.

'Anything can stimulate an idea - art, the colour of stones or the stitching and seaming on a handbag. I

The Tigre D'or.

like to apply something you see or an idea in a different way by taking it completely out of context.'

The main saloon on the Sea Sedan.

Eren Yorulmazer

Designer: Eren Yorulmazer. **Company:** Eren Yorulmazer, Turkey. **Work:** Both houses and restaurants - more than 140 in the last eight years. **Signature:** Modern, but in a way that combines yesterday, today and tomorrow. **Colour:** My basic colours start with white and end with ecru and I love to add black, purple and red. While I do not like colourful objects, I do like fabrics in strong colours. **Best idea:** Doing this job. **Big break:** Being brave and having my own style. It is vital to be freethinking. **Biggest influence:** The history of fashion. I read about fashion designers lives and pore over their work. At the moment, I am reading about John Galliano and Jean Paul Gaultier. **Motivation:** Designing what I feel, not what I think. When I finish a job, I only want to hear the word 'wow'. **New directions:** As time passes, things change, but only a little. **Favourite painting:** The Sabine Women (1799) by Jacques Louis David. It has everything... war, royalty, fashion, people and colour. **Favourite movie star:** Sophia Loren. She is the epitome of a Mediterranean woman and when I look at her I feel human. **Favourite country:** Italy, because whenever I visit, I feel alive. **Free time:** Photography and collecting books. **Top shop:** The New York furniture and accessories store, Alan Moss and Colette in Paris for the mix of stylish pieces and fashion. **Pet hates:** Plastic things and strong light used in the wrong way.

'It is vital to be freethinking and different.'

Entrance to house on the Bosporus, Istanbul.

TMH Designs

Designers: Karen Howes and Gail Taylor. **Company:** TMH Designs, London. **Work:** High-calibre show flats, residential projects and health spas. **Signature:** Adding the 'wow' factor, value-for-money and originality. **Colour:** Rather than using vast tracts of colour on the walls, we use colour as an accent to neutral tones. That could be a glazed aubergine pot or a duck egg blue cushion, but we always try to give people colours that are slightly ahead of the game. **Best idea:** Working as a team. **Big break:** Moving to Chelsea Harbour Design Centre has made us feel very connected to the rest of the industry. **Biggest influence:** Karen and I have worked together for over ten years and we are extremely good friends, so she is my biggest influence and I am hers. **Motivation:** Never knowing what the day will bring - I have always loved that about my job. **New directions:** Our whole team always thinks about what has not been seen before, but changes are subliminal and our work

develops naturally day by day rather than taking a sudden leap in a new direction. **Favourite painting:** Water Pots in the Thar Desert, by Sarah Jane Hocking, which I own. It's quite ethnic and shows the back view of two Indian ladies wearing saris, carrying water on their heads. It is a magical and uplifting painting. **Favourite movie star:** Steve McQueen - he is so cool. **Favourite country:** Karen dreams of retiring to a hilltop in Tuscany

and I love the Far East for the culture and the people, but whenever either of us returns home to England, we feel this is the best place because of the changing seasons. **Free time:** Our kids (both of us are working mums). And sleep. **Top shop:** Donna Karan in Bond Street both for the clothes and her fantastic ceramic pots. **Pet hates:** Retro design, whether that is on cars, interiors or fashion. We have had all that and I don't want to see it again.

'We use colour as an accent, not a major statement.'

'Your interior is as important as your clothes or cars.'

JBA Interiors

Designer: Diane Fasce Meleski and John Blatteau. **Company:** JBA Interiors, Philadelphia, USA. **Work:** A mix of residential and institutional. I am an architect and Diane is an interior designer. **Signature:** A fresh honest approach to classical and traditional interiors. It is literal classicism without being a pastiche. **Colour:** Generally, our interior palette has both deep and bright colours as they have majesty and strength, which is appropriate to the design. Sometimes the colour is on the wall, others in the draperies with lush fabrics and damasks. **Best idea:** This partnership. It has been a great collaboration for the past 20 years. **Big break:** The real issue is being ready for the break. When we designed the diplomatic reception rooms for The United States Department of State in Washington - the rooms are a forum to display 18th and 19th century American decorative arts - the work gave us a national stage and access to another level of client. **Biggest influence:** One of our favourite houses is a Villa called Kerylos in the south of France. It is a fantastic recreation of a Greek villa built in the twenties. **Motivation:** Our clients... we don't have clients who are uninvolved. And beauty. It is the reward for all the effort. **New directions:** We don't experiment with novelty in architecture, but we are always looking for ways of investing something new into something that has existed for 2,500 years.

We try to extend classical language and style to create a balance between permanence and innovation. **Favourite painting:** The Architects Dream by Thomas Cole. It is a great metaphor for what was happening in America in the 1830s. The painter is sprawled on a Doric Column with rolls of drawings and he is looking out over a river where there are sunlit classical buildings on one side and shadowy Gothic on the other. The point was to illustrate that at that time, people were breaking away from Gothic and opening up to a new urban experience. **Favourite movie star:** Katherine Hepburn had real style. **Favourite country:** The French represent the classic ideal and I go to Paris every year... and Diane loves Italy. Each year, she spends a month in Venice. **Free time:** Cooking and gardening... and watercolour painting. **Top shop:** ABC Home. There must be seven floors of everything from antiques to linen, furniture, dishes, fresh flowers and more... it is like a department store without the clothes. **Pet hates:** An uninvolved client. And the very strong modernist look as it is too harsh and not human.

'We are not into ironic plays on style.'

The diplomatic reception room for the US Department of State, Washington DC.

Joseph Sy & Associates

Designer: Joseph Sy. **Company:** Joseph Sy & Associates, Hong Kong. **Work:** Both residential and commercial, mainly in Hong Kong and China. **Signature:** Making workable spaces that are as simple as possible. **Colour:** While I do use off-whites, I am moving toward using pastels such as turquoise and earth tones and greens, because they calm and cool down the ambience in a room. I have become tired of chocolate brown, which has been the fashion for the past few years, and I am replacing it with light coloured woods and working on bleaching and staining to enhance woodgrain. **Best idea:** Using moving walls or screens to create multi-functional spaces that also maximise the space - particularly relevant in Hong Kong. **Big break:** Completing a huge 5,000 square meter restaurant in Guangzhou in China. It is totally different from conventional restaurants and has had a great deal of publicity. **Biggest influence:** Space and light and everything I see. **Motivation:** The real drive is the challenge and the willingness to do what is right for the job.

New directions: Moving toward colour and greater comfort. **Favourite painting:** No one in particular; any of Miro's line drawings that are like a child's work. **Favourite movie star:** Anthony Hopkins is a brilliant actor and is quite fascinating. **Favourite country:** Japan - they have that extreme of modern and traditional working side by side. **Free time:** I work Monday to Sunday... and listening to music. **Top shop:** Any export outlets as I don't really have time to shop. **Pet hates:** Over-doing things on any level and clutter.

'Comfort is more honest than glamour. Every interior should be comfortable.'

Jorge A Lacarra

Designer: Jorge A Lacarra. **Company:** Creation Cycle, Rome, Italy. **Work:** Homes, hotels, offices and furniture design. **Signature:** Adding energy to a space and changing peoples' lives. **Colour:** Colour always depends on the light and space. I don't use bright colours if there is a lot of light outside. I love all the African colours - browns, beige, greens - and the oranges, greens and yellows of Tibet. But light is the most important thing in my decoration. **Best idea:** Using fabric glued directly onto the painted walls to create borders within the room. I sometimes even cover the doors with fabric. It's effect is three-dimensional and rich. **Big break:** I was a theatre designer and my first job was in Argentina. I did a boutique, then a restaurant and then an apartment. Step by step I left the theatre and became a decorator. The next break was moving to Italy over 25 years ago.

Biggest influence: The theatre. And the late David Hicks - he changed taste in general. **Motivation:** The client. I work very hard for them, as hard is the only way to work. **New directions:** Colour. I like to discover new colours. Each season, I take a little bit of what is best from general trends and the catwalks. **Favourite painting:** The Red Fish by Matisse is magic. **Favourite movie star:** Rita Hayworth. She was so beautiful and glamorous, but I also love her for the way she moved and talked. **Favourite country:** No one in particular; I love the world. **Free time:** Being with friends, the theatre, listening to music, reading, designing, meditation and being alone. **Top shop:** A little bookshop in Rome, called Libreria Borghese. I buy art books and novels and visit twice a month just to see what is in stock. **Pet hates:** I don't like pretentiousness or things being there for the sake of it and I hate cold-looking places that are without soul.

'Everything should be sensual, even in an office. Nothing should be cold or lack soul.'

'To have a free, open space
in an apartment is a real
luxury.'

Lifestyles Interiors

Designer: Helen Green. **Company:** Lifestyles Interiors, London **Work:** Both residential and commercial projects. **Signature:** Modern classical with more than a hint of glamour - I always strive for elegance. **Colour:** Colour is back for sure, because it is the foil to the classic neutral background. We develop the picture in layers rather like a painting against a neutral background. The colour really comes into the finishes such as joinery and accessories like glassware. **Best idea:** Living in a monastic space while my house was being renovated. It clarified my mind and gave me breathing space. **Big break:** Forming an association with the developers, Northacre plc in 1995. It has given us a great deal of work and excellent exposure. **Biggest influence:** Travel. **Motivation:** Challenge. That is the best motivation. **New directions:** There is no question that people want more glamour as we are all bored with the monastic minimalist look. We all want to be inspired. **Favourite painting:** Femme et Singes (Woman and Monkeys) by Henri Matisse. It is highly abstract, but at the same time figurative. It comes back to having the best of both worlds. **Favourite movie star:** Lauren Baccal. She is classy, sexy, svelte and she's got character. **Favourite country:** changes from year to year... but United States of America offers everything. **Free time:** Don't have it. **Top shop:** The new General Trading Company. It has everything, plus a totally international feel. **Pet hates:** Anything that lacks soul... a space, a building, a dinner party...

'Everyone is trying to go through that transition from classical to contemporary... it gives you the best of both worlds and leaves you with an inspired but comfortable interior.'

'An elegant, glamorous look
can be tempered up or
down, so it could work for a
traditionalist just as it could
be made to work for
someone who wants a
more modern slant.'

Steve Leung Designers Limited

Designer: Steve Leung. **Company:** Steve Leung Designers Limited, Hong Kong. **Work:** Architectural and interior projects for private and commercial schemes including club houses, offices, restaurants and bars. **Signature:** Minimal but not minimalist. My kind of minimalism is expressed with character and culture. **Colour:** Bright green and orange are two colours I use, but very carefully and always with neutrals. The basics are black, brown and beige, and white is very friendly... no one objects to white. **Best idea:** Travelling to villages in China for inspiration - some of these places are 2,000 years old and are comparable to any Italian city. **Big break:** While I was at University, I set myself the target of starting my own practice and my first job under my own name came six years later, when I built an extension for a school. Since then during the past four years, I have designed over 50 private homes. **Biggest influence:** China... it is so rich in terms of culture. I am driven by being Chinese and living in a Chinese society and am in love with the Asian culture in China. The quadrangle houses and garden courtyards with verandas are truly inspiring. **Motivation:** The finished product. When I, or any of my staff look back at our work it drives us on to do more. **New directions:** My ambition is to derive a minimal, romantic style that carries an Oriental flavour. **Favourite painting:** Any of the abstract works by the Chinese artist Zao Wou-Ki. Some are bright, others very dark, and there is always something to see within the canvas. **Favourite movie star:** Steve Martin. **Favourite country:** Next to China, it must be Italy. I like the intimacy and the feeling that every time you turn a corner you find something different. **Free time:** Playing golf and going to galleries. **Top shop:** Jil Sander in Berlin. It is a very comfortable place to shop with exciting product. **Pet hates:** Anything pretentious or clumsy... and too much layering in a design or very classical style.

'My ambition is to derive a minimal, romantic style that carries an Oriental flavour.'

'A residential project is not just about
design, it is a communication challenge as
everybody living there must be happy. Here,
this isn't just the husband and wife and
children, often it includes the grandparents
as well.'

David Carter

Designer: David Carter. **Company:** David Carter Interior Decorator, London. **Work:** Almost exclusively residential. **Signature:** Being overtly theatrical... and playful. My work is not at all minimal. It has a three dimensional quality that has been described as being 'Alice Through The Looking Glass'. **Colour:** I use colour a lot and love the transition of one space moving into another. I work with extremes: sometimes with Gustavian colours that have that sun-bleached look that has an almost ghostlike quality, or working with very saturated pigments such as inky indigos, very dense greens and strong reds. **Best idea:** Using artists canvas almost like sails as conservatory blinds instead of those horrid blinds from conservatory companies. Mine were painted with a kind of Roman orgy theme. **Big break:** Back in 1991, The World of Interiors photographed my old flat and it appeared on the front cover. That opened a door for me and I knew if I wanted to be a decorator I could do it. My first job was a dental surgery. **Biggest influence:** The French designer, Andre Arbus. He worked during the twenties and thirties, but his main time was the forties. His work is sort of classic but contemporary and it is amazingly stylish, with a grand feeling that has a dangerous, decadent quality. **Motivation:** Survival. **New directions:** None, just carry on doing my own work. **Favourite painting:** Boldini's portrait of Lady Colin Campbell. It is so very sexy. **Favourite movie star:** Jean Louis Barroult... the star of some amazing French films. He could communicate with just a look. **Favourite country:** France. **Free time:** My two very demanding young children are my major recreation. **Top shop:** Alfie's Antique Market in London. **Pet hates:** Wallpaper. No matter how expensive the paper, or how well it is hung, you are always aware of the seams.

'My work is quite theatrical,
so my dream job would be
to design an exotic brothel.'

'It fascinates me that decoration can affect people to such an extent. My ultimate goal is to Carterise everything.'

ek Reedy Interiors Inc

Designer: Katherine Reedy. **Company:** ek Reedy Interiors Inc. Wyoming, USA. **Work:** Mostly high-end residential with some commercial work such as boutiques and restaurants. **Signature:** Our work is reflective of a regional, mountain area and we focus on creating spaces that become a whole way of living. We are known for our lighting, use of colour and materials. **Colour:** White does not work in this part of the world, as there is snow for nearly six months of the year. Sage green is a predominant natural colour in the landscape and we use a lot of it with natural wheat tones. Every now and then we jazz up those colours with red. We also use a lot of tinted Venetian plaster - it gives a wall more life, because it is not a monotone finish. **Best idea:** Creating a whole ceiling structure in a room with a 25 feet high ceiling. It was designed to house the lighting but it also improved the proportion of the room and gave it movement. **Big break:** There has been no one big break, just a series of stepping-stones. All our work comes through recommendations. **Biggest influence:** Architecture in general. **Motivation:** Firstly, what can be created and then seeing the work finished. **New directions:** Designing a product line... upholstery, lighting, tableware and so on... **Favourite painting:** Haystacks by Van Gogh. It has such emotion, colour and texture. **Favourite movie star:** Al Pacino. He is not the most attractive actor, but he always plays his characters convincingly. **Favourite country:** Italy for design, architecture, food, shoes and cars. **Free time:** Skiing, fly fishing and taking nice long walks. **Top shop:** Holly Hunt in New York and an antiques shop in Denver called Eron Johson that sells a great mix of things from all over the place. **Pet hates:** A drab interior, or an interior that is so done that it is no fun at all.

'Lighting gives a room its atmosphere, but a great interior is one that you respond to again and again because of the forms and sizes of the various pieces. They generate activity.'

'Because we have six months of snow, colour is vital. White does not work in this part of the world. Our neutrals are colours like sage green and golden wheat tones.'

Associates III

Designers: Kari Foster, Annette Stelmack, Maggie Tandysh, Beth Scott, Anne Hemsi, Angie Pache and Donna Barta-Winfield. **Company:** Associates III, Denver, Colorado, USA. **Work:** Mainly residential work such as mini palaces in Saudi Arabia and a log home in Japan, plus commercial projects. **Signature:** Creating a home not a house. Our approach is to be open and to find the right solution for each project, so we therefore don't have a particular style. **Colour:** Colour always depends on the client, but we tend to create shells that are timeless and neutral through the use of natural materials. Greens and reds work well here because they are warm and balance the snow. **Best idea:** Working as a team and really listening to the client. **Big break:** Designing boutique hotels and in particular, The Hyatt Regency in Beaver Creek. We got a lot of public exposure and people loved the fact that the work had a very residential feeling. We were subsequently asked to create homes that looked like hotels.

Biggest influence: Each other... and the environment. How do we solve the problem of designing and creating and still be kind to the earth. **Motivation:** Being the glue that holds all the various elements of a project together from the client to the architect to the craftsmen. **New directions:** There is always something new or fresh to discover or rediscover, but it always comes back to what the client wants. **Favourite painting:** There are too many of us to pick one favourite painting, but we all love any Van Gogh or Picasso and all of the work by our local artists,

Cheryl Derrick and William Matthews. **Favourite movie star:** Benecio del Toro... he was great in Traffic, is incredibly sexy and has great eyes. **Favourite country:** Italy, for the romance, the sense of history, the landscape, the architecture, the people and the food. **Free time:** All of us like getting out to the outdoors. **Top shop:** Takashimaya in New York is impeccable. Everything is exquisite and the store is so restrained and intimate. **Pet hates:** Lack of respect for the environment, arrogance and pretentiousness, and misconceptions about design and the word decorator.

'People respond to our work with words like fun, home, creative.'

'We were asked to create
homes that looked like
hotels.'

Lannis Peta Spiro Interiors

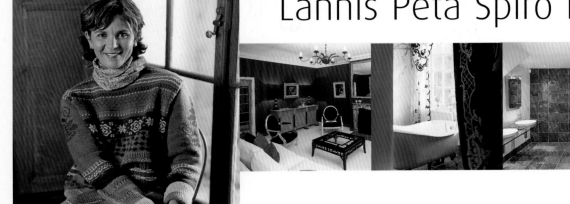

Designer: Lannis Spiro. **Company:** Lannis Peta Spiro Interiors, Britain. **Work:** Mainly residential projects done in conjunction with developers. **Signature:** Opening up a house rather than compartmentalising it... and bringing the outdoors inside. **Colour:** I use neutrals to create a calm background, but I am affected by what is going on in fashion on the street. I will always have a splash of some sort - a brilliant painting, one chair that has nothing to do with the rest of the colour palette and so on. **Best idea:** Partitioning off an area of a room to get away from using wardrobes. It is as good a way of creating storage within a space, as it is a walk-in dressing room within a bedroom. **Big break:** While I was on holiday, a friend introduced me to the director of a development company. I was hired on the basis of the clothes I was wearing and it was the beginning of a large number of new-build house projects for me. **Biggest influence:** Living in South Africa...

the beach... the sea... African art... the use of stone... the way art is so totally uncontrived and oversized.... **Motivation:** The pure love of creating something from nothing. I love that thing of starting with a square box and creating something. **New directions:** Generally going a bit soft, even with colours and building houses on beaches. **Favourite painting:** A huge turquoise and aquamarine painting called Peacock, by the British artist, Jane Landes. In her paintings, she uses fabrics mixed with heavily brushed oils, which somehow makes them look as though they are flowing. I have her work all over my house. **Favourite movie star:** Morgan

Freeman. He has the most unbelievable, earthy, powerful voice. No matter what the film, I will go to listen to him. **Favourite country:** South Africa for everything from the beaches to the music. It makes me come alive. **Free time:** Being Mum. **Top shop:** A shop on Madison Avenue called McKenzies-Child - there are beads set into bowls and broken stones in the lamps and a whole mix of materials and things that you don't expect to see. It is just outrageous. **Pet hates:** Cushions that match the curtains and anything that dictates or is so finished that it doesn't leave room for later additions. On a fashion level, jumpers that are tucked into trousers.

'Every time I return from South Africa, I am bombarded by the idea of bringing Africa into my house in every possible way that I can.'

Alberto Pinto

Designer: Alberto Pinto. **Company:** Alberto Pinto, Paris, France. **Work:** Both residential and commercial work that includes private boats and planes, hotels, homes and ranches. **Signature:** Working with, not against a building's architecture, to create a grandiose first impression and turning details into works of art. I don't specialise in any particular look. It is not a problem for me to go from Louis XV to modern. **Colour:** I use colour to both enhance the architecture of the building and to tame the natural light. **Best idea:** Hiring Olivier, one of the best Parisian chefs, to prepare luncheons at the office. **Big break:** At the age of 20, Ms Rosemary Kanzler gave me full liberty to decorate her residence in Saint Jean Cap Ferrat on the French Riviera. **Biggest influence:** The interior designer, David Hicks and the architect, Luis Baragan. **Motivation:** My work gets me up in the morning. **New directions:** Launching new lines of home accessories like the Cristobal porcelain tableware with Raynaud Limoges. **Favourite painting:** Les Menines by Velasquez. **Favourite movie star:** Betty Boop. **Favourite country:** I am at home in both the USA and France, living with one foot in New York and the other in Paris. **Free time:** I am a shopping addict. **Top shop:** Kirk & Rosie Rich, Rue de la Tremouille, Paris... **Pet hates:** To have to dine out.

'A house has to match the personality of its owner. It has to look alive.'

'I use colour to tame the natural light.'

A ranch in Santa Fe, New Mexico.

'I am known for my opulent interiors, but this is not all I do... the skill is adapting many styles from many periods to create a look that suits the client's wishes.'

Alssamoure Design Associates

Designer: Sara A. Al Faisal. **Company:** Alssamoure Design Associates, Saudi Arabia. **Work:** Both interior and architectural work that includes homes and commercial work. **Signature:** Creating atmosphere and a sense of elegance that is very sophisticated. **Colour:** In an Islamic culture, people want vibrant, strong colours. It is very rare that a client will ask for neutrals. I use strong reds and gold, but in such a way that is stylish and not at all gaudy. These, mixed with blue, green and purple create a modern, atmospheric interior. **Best idea:** Using Islamic colours in a contemporary interior. And doing a Masters degree in Design Management - that has improved my business tremendously as people now look at us as being design professionals rather than as artists or decorators. **Big break:** Winning two very large projects in Saudi Arabia: one was a large private residence for a member of the royal family and the other, a contemporary Islamic palace. I was trusted blindly in terms of taste and all our work has followed from that. **Biggest influence:** Art Deco furniture and

Islamic art. **Motivation:** Seeing something in your head and then actually realising it. If I were not an interior designer, I would probably be a carpenter. **New directions:** Allowing contemporary design to evolve in this environment. Now everybody in Saudi Arabia is open to contemporary design mixed with classical elements, whereas as little as five years ago, that would have been impossible. **Favourite painting:** A three-panel piece by the British artist Tony Reason that I

bought in New York. It is real rust on paper and looks like a very beautiful sunset. It is a very soothing piece of work. **Favourite movie star:** Helen Mirren is the best actress under the sun. **Favourite country:** Saudi Arabia. It is my home. **Free time:** When I get any, I read historical novels. **Top shop:** The design centres in New York. **Pet hates:** Poor quality work of any kind and bad finishing. I also hate Plexiglas, as it is a horrid material that ages badly and scratches.

'We are good at interpretations and have
had to find a style that can carry collections
of Art Deco and Islamic rugs.'

'Our interiors are atmospheric: when you walk in you will get the feeling of both nostalgia and comfort.'

Lantis-Bain Scorgie

Designer: Lantis-Bain Scorgie. **Company:** Lantis-Bain Scorgie, Johannesburg, South Africa. **Work:** Mainly residential projects, mixed with some commercial work such as game lodges and hotels. **Signature:** Being quirky... I tend to work monochromatically and dramatically. I like to work with things that I have found rather than with things that I have looked for. But more than anything, I use what my client already owns so that I do not decorate away their personality. **Colour:** I am not a colourful person and a lot of my work is very dark. If I do use a bright colour I will only use one at a time. Right now, flies eye green, a bright chartreuse tone, looks perfect with charcoal because it is off-the-wall and exciting. **Best idea:** Returning to South Africa to set up this business, after having lived in London. **Big break:** Designing the

game lodge, Chitwa Chitwa in the Sabi Sands in 1996. The design was completely lunatic and over the top with lots of gold leaf, reds and yellows and all the bedrooms were in dark charcoal. Many of the people who stayed at the lodge became clients. **Biggest influence:** Travel. Everything I see gets computed and then spat back out in some way. **Motivation:** I love what I do. **New directions:** Adding opulence. Fabrics need to be completely patterned and romance has to come back into interiors and that includes that whole inherited look. Everyone who threw out his or her furniture to live minimally now has

to go out and inherit it again. **Favourite painting:** Any Pop Art, by Andy Warhol and Keith Harring. I like it because it is not important; it is just there just like wallpaper. **Favourite movie star:** Richard E Grant (the only person whose books I read) and Sandra Bernard. She is a lunatic woman with a great big mouth. **Favourite country:** Italy - I have been so many times and I have such wonderful friends. **Free time:** What free time? **Top shop:** Takashimaya in New York. It is so new and the approach to the product is so different. **Pet hates:** Things that match and bad proportions.

'I like working with things that I have found, rather than with things that I have looked for.'

'I use dark colours, and tend to work monochromatically, but not in a morbid or sombre way. My kind of dark is restful and works especially well in Africa because there is so much sunlight.'

Decollo Interior Design

Designer: Jo Archibald. **Company:** Decollo Interior Design, Victoria, Australia. **Work:** Both residential and commercial. **Signature:** Creating a relaxed look where texture and quality are paramount. I don't like being locked into a particular look, because I take inspiration from the individual brief. I like to use a mixture of both antique and contemporary textiles that have a balance of colour and, or texture. **Colour:** I like to use colour in pattern and texture, not as a solid block. Red is a favourite as it adds contrast to neutrals and is very comforting. **Best idea:** Using things in a fresh way such as taking the pages from old Japanese scholars' textbooks and pasting them on the wall as wallpaper. I did this in a powder room and the effect was stunning. **Big break:** The transition from fabric designer and manufacturer to interior designer by way of supportive clients who asked me to decorate their homes with my

fabrics. **Biggest influence:** My mother, who taught me the appreciation of creative and beautiful things... and travel. **Motivation:** Creating a comfortable home, not a pretentious showplace. **New directions:** Every client takes you in a new direction because of their different personalities, needs and styles. Last year I was involved in the interior design of a golf clubhouse and enjoyed the challenge of using products that were durable enough to withstand constant use and wear and tear from golf shoes etc... **Favourite painting:** I cannot name a particular painting, however I do love paintings from the twenties and

thirties by the artists Duncan Grant, George Bell and Grace Cossington-Smith. **Favourite movie star:** I have no favourite actor, but Sean Connery seems to be a charming man. **Favourite country:** Australia - as a New Zealander it has been very good to me. But I love to travel to Italy for the colours, the people and the food. **Free time:** Reading, drawing, playing golf and being with my family and friends. **Top shop:** Christian Liaigre in Paris - I envy the discipline of its elegance and refined style. **Pet hates:** Cushions that are positioned so they sit on their points or so the zippers show.

'Red often appears as an accent not as a solid colour.'

'My ideal room would be a space with lots of textured fabrics a wonderfully comfortable sofa, an open fireplace and a view of a rugged coastline.'

Emanuel Gomes

Designer: Emanuel Gomes. **Company:** Emanuel Gomes M, Lisbon, Portugal. **Work:** Both residential and commercial work that includes shops and offices. **Signature:** If anything, it is making the budget, the use of the money, however large or small, shine out. I don't have a specific style. I am like a chameleon and take on the clients' colours. **Colour:** I like every single colour, but I don't use colour in a strong way. There are so many things that grab and shout for your attention that it makes sense to use softer, more dilute colours in our homes, as they are less demanding on the eye. **Best idea:** Being open to absolutely everybody and everything. My attitude has been that a home is either a palace or a little cottage. It is a nest that varies in quality according to our lifestyle. **Big break:** Continuous study. I studied during the mid-seventies at New York School of Interior Design and plan to return to do a Masters degree next year even though I have been a

designer for 26 years. In between, I have studied architecture, interior design, sociology, social anthropology... **Biggest influence:** People. **Motivation:** The illusion. Am I capable of making the dream come true on each job? **New directions:** My ideology is to work toward understanding how to build a space for anyone, independent of their social strata. **Favourite painting:** A large 2m by 1.6m canvas by Pedro Casqueiro. The composition is squares and rectangles of colour, arranged to

look like a piece of cloth. **Favourite movie star:** Both Glenn Close and Meryl Streep. They are strong women who show their emotions. **Favourite country:** The United Kingdom. It is civilised and I like the way the people look at life. **Free time:** Study. **Top shop:** Hamley's in London. Every time I visit, I spend hours taking in the toys... toys have an enormous influence on me because I am fascinated by the materials, the innovation and the colours. **Pet hates:** Lack of balance.

'For me there is no good taste or bad taste.'

'There are so many things in life that grab and
shout for your attention, it makes sense to use
softer, more dilute colours in our homes.'

Petra Schlapp Interiors

Designer: Petra Schlapp. **Company:** Petra Schlapp Interiors, Frankfurt, London and New York. **Work:** Mainly residential with occasional commercial projects. **Signature:** Creating a warm, eclectic atmosphere that is sophisticated, elegant and traditional. **Colour:** I love earthy tones that are more brown than terracotta - chocolate, caramel, warm grey tones and shades of cream, sometimes with an accent of aubergine - and use them to make a home feel warm. But colour depends on the house and its environment. Traditional houses need colours like deep reds, yellows and blues, while apartments that are not architecturally traditional, work in all the colours between chocolate and cream. **Best**

idea: Becoming an interior designer eight years ago. **Big break:** My first commercial job was a private bank in Hamburg and the first residential project, a home in London, but the real break is always word of mouth and being in the right place at the right time. **Biggest influence:** Travel. It makes you appreciate things in a different way, even if you are not conscious of it at the time. **Motivation:** To make a house feel like a home. **New directions:** What I do always comes back to what the client wants and the location of the house. **Favourite painting:** The amazing,

grand frescos by the seventeenth century painter, Tiepolo. **Favourite movie star:** Audrey Hepburn. She had immense grace and style and was always the perfect lady. **Favourite country:** Italy. I love the culture and the Italian way of living, the food, the language and the incredible history of the buildings. **Free time:** Spending time with people who are important to me. **Top shop:** Barney's in New York for the variety and the top designer names. It is just so up to date. **Pet hates:** Cold colours and materials, people I cannot rely on and bad workmanship.

'That worldwide, international feeling comes from the mix of traditional European design blended with elements from Asian, African and other cultures.'

'It is exciting to bring together two very contrasting things. It works precisely because the elements don't match.'

KSR Clifton

Designer: Mark Ruthven and Rosie Winston. **Company:** KSR Clifton, London. **Work:** Working collaboratively for the past five years - one of us is an interior designer, the other an architect. Projects include new buildings for developers. **Signature:** Contemporary in a classic manner, with an emphasis on natural materials. **Colour:** Natural materials create the colour and off whites are a helpful device to establish contrast, but we like to punctuate neutral interiors with strong colours, such as bold terracotta and green. **Best idea:** This partnership. Working together from the beginning of a project gives the client many benefits, including continuity and harmony. **Big break:** Two substantial house projects gave us the opportunity to try more experimental ideas like using glass, leather and timber in combination... and the work we have done over the past three years on The Pavilion next to Lords Cricket Ground. That was very challenging as the space is enormous with 120 apartments. **Biggest influence:** Light. It affects everything. **Motivation:** Working together and with other people to see what we can really do and developing ideas with clients in a way they had not thought about before. Ultimately, it is to produce beautiful homes. **New directions:** To extend ourselves and work beyond the residential market. **Favourite painting:** Any painting by Howard Hodgson, for the colour and the way he extends the paint beyond the canvas onto the frame... and Starry Nights by Van Gogh for the drama. **Favourite movie star:** Bette Davis is bizarre, eccentric and one of the greatest... and Charlie Chaplin. **Favourite country:** India is breathtaking. **Free time:** What free time. We both have kids. **Top shop:** Patisserie Valerie - it's our haunt, for pain au chocolat or anything with chocolate. **Pet hates:** Lack of time.

'Working in collaboration makes perfect sense as the architecture and interior design become more harmonious - the two disciplines are not seen as separate exercises, they become part of one another.'

Gluckstein Design

Designer: Brian Gluckstein. **Company:** Gluckstein Design, Toronto. **Work:** Residential and commercial projects, plus the recent launch of a bedlinen and accessories collection. **Signature:** There is an eclectic mix in our spaces. A modern space will always have a classical element and vice versa. **Colour:** Our colours tend to be greyed like smoky blues, celadon greens, creamy yellows and brick reds. Even the softest colours are smoky and we often have to mix them ourselves. They are somewhat influenced by colour trends although we are known for a very natural palette. **Best idea:** Apart from getting into this business... it must have been to put books into a bathroom. It is such a natural idea to have a wall of books near the tub. It is the perfect combination. **Big break:** Two of my first clients were art collectors and the subsequent exposure was huge and instantaneous. The clients were known for extraordinary good taste and that gave us a lot of credibility. **Biggest influence:** Reading...

and travelling. From an early age travel exposed me to another level and opened my eyes to another sense. **Motivation:** Trying new things... design, materials and so on. I always push, but not to a degree where it gets wacky. **New directions:** there is no particular direction, but I find that the spaces are becoming more mature. The work gets better and more refined with age. **Favourite painting:** I own it - a fantastic painting called Art in America by David Bierk. It's about six and a half feet high and four feet wide and is divided into two panels. The left section is a

reproduction of a magazine cover and on the right has a little Monet painting behind a piece of glass. It is fantastic. **Favourite movie star:** Cary Grant. I love his style, the way he dressed and how he carried himself. **Favourite country:** Canada - parts of it are geographically miraculous. And I love Italy. **Free time:** Reading in my bathtub and trawling through antique markets. **Top shop:** William Yeoward in London. One of the things I covet for my own home is William Yeoward's stemware. **Pet hates:** Clutter, arrogance and pretentiousness.

'There is always a certain cleanness in our work, even though we rarely design a space that is in one period or style.'

'Everybody wants good design; every age group wants great surroundings. This is something that is very new and it has evolved during the past decade. Even people going off to University want a beautiful space.'

Azul-Tierra

Designer: Toni Espuch. **Company:** Azul-Tierra, Alicante, Spain. **Work:** Hotels, restaurants and private homes in Spain, England, Italy, France and Tunisia. **Signature:** Creating ambience and warmth using a mix of old and new. **Colour:** Natural colours create a good background and the inherent colours in the materials - stone, wood etc - create the special colour moments. I like chocolate and brown tones, and reds and clarets because they are warm. This would work in a rural setting whereas I would choose a more white based palette if the house was by the sea. **Best idea:** The project that has just been completed - you can see how all the ideas have evolved and moved on. Each job grows from the previous job. **Big break:** There has been no one break. I have worked tremendously hard for the past 11 years. **Biggest influence:** Travel. **Motivation:** The magic of creating another world. This job is like a hobby and I love getting the job done and seeing the finished result. **New directions:** Allowing the work to evolve in every way, every day. I am always trying to create a new mix using influences from recent travels. **Favourite painting:** The paintings in general by the thirties painter, Gustav Klimt. His work is very modern and he uses wonderful gold colours. **Favourite movie star:** It depends on my mood... but whenever I watch a Bette Davis movie I am always impressed by the way she moves, laughs and the general mood that she creates on the screen. **Favourite country:** My roots are in Spain and it is a beautiful country... and India for the people, the mood and the colours. **Free time:** Travelling and thinking through ideas. My work is like my hobby. **Top shop:** A shop in Madrid called Pascua Ortega that sells a quirky mix of both antique and new interior products. **Pet hates:** Everything kitsch.

'Design can be like magic... you close the door behind you having entered another world.'

'It is the mood, the overall warmth and atmosphere that bring a space alive. That is more important than any other aspect of interior design.'

Hare & Klein

Designer: Meryl Hare. **Company:** Hare & Klein, Sydney, Australia. **Work:** Both private and commercial residential work all over Australia. **Signature:** Using a mix of styles and a combination of scale, texture and colour done in such a way that is right for the client, but which does not have the obvious stamp of an interior designer. **Colour:** My colours tend to be understated, leaning toward tones like aubergine, terracotta, charcoal, pistachio and an ivory that is slightly greyed. I always see black as a sharp 'bright' colour as it lifts other colours... and I love it when there is a colour in a room for no obvious good reason. **Best** **idea:** Being an interior designer full stop. **Big break:** Generosity of spirit from clients who pass on your name. **Biggest influence:** Africa - I grew up in Zambia, Swaziland and South Africa - and travel. **Motivation:** Each job. The blank canvas. The painting of a picture. Making something lovely. **New directions:** There are always fresh ideas, increased by technology and communication... you have to keep riding the horse or it will bolt. **Favourite painting:** A Castle for King Lear, by Margaret Vorster. I love it because it is mad and I look at it every day. It is a large canvas in wild reds, blues, black and yellow and appears to have a tree and a path and some clouds. **Favourite movie star:** Mel Gibson. He can act, he is very sexy and he has wonderfully intense eyes. **Favourite country:** I love India, as it is unbelievably spiritual and rich in colour and texture. I also think that I will love Egypt, but I have not been there yet. **Free time:** Going to all sorts of places with my two daughters, travel such as bicycling throughout Vietnam with my husband. **Top shop:** You don't have to buy anything to go shopping, so I would choose Fortuny in Venice, because everything is incredible. **Pet hates:** Pretentiousness and anything that is too self-conscious.

Jestico & Whiles

Designers: John Whiles, Tony Ingram, Tony Ling, James Dilley, David Perera, Michelle le Masurier and Sniez Torbarina. **Company:** Jestico & Whiles, London. **Work:** Both residential and commercial projects such as spas and hotels that include The Hempel and One Aldwych. **Signature:** First and foremost, it's modern - elegant, stylish, witty, warm and intuitive. **Colour:** There are no set rules as we work intuitively in each new situation. Each of us loves colour, but we like to be sparse with it so that when we do apply colour the effect is very strong. **Best idea:** Working as a team... from the beginning of every job, we start with a joint vision of the ultimate aim. There is a tremendous sense of balance and fluidity in the work because our team comprises both architects and interior designers. **Big break:** One Aldwych. It was a complete project where we had to look at every corner, every detail, every aspect... And then creating the warmth and wit for Malmaison hotels in Birmingham and Edinburgh at a time when there were no other hotels in that league. **Biggest influence:** Le Corbusier is important to us all... the Irish designer, Eileen Grey, for her elegant and simple work and the interior and furniture designer, Jean-Michel Frank. **Motivation:** The end result. **New directions:** Not only creating interiors and buildings, but to create a whole brand image for our clients. **Favourite painting:** There are too many of us to choose one painting, but I like Gary Hume's paintings. I own a sketch he did last year that shows the outline of a landscape that is almost abstract. **Favourite movie star:** Any stylish actor of any time like Audrey Hepburn, Catherine Deneuve and Steve McQueen... it is not just their looks, it is everything about them. **Favourite country:** Italy is a joy. We all enjoy Italy for its art and architecture and it is also culturally strong in modern design and has always been so. **Free time:** As a team, we all enjoy playing softball in Regents Park in the Spring. **Top shop:** There are many lovely shops, but there is not one that I would say is the greatest. **Pet hates:** Looking at design in an isolated way.

'We are a team of both architects and designers and as a result, there is a tremendous sense of balance and fluidity in our work. From the beginning of every job, we start with a joint vision of the ultimate aim.'

Washrooms at Village Cinemas in Cerny Most, top and staircase at One Aldwych, right.

'We use colour sparingly as
we don't wish to devalue
its importance.'

Moe & lena

Designer: Mads Moe. **Company:** Moe & lena, Oslo, Norway. **Work:** Both commercial and residential, plus offices that are more like a home. **Signature:** Classic contemporary with a twist. I like to add the unexpected element. **Colour:** Brownish taupe is a favourite neutral because it is rich, not too dark and is a great foil to modern art and I also use a lot of creams and greys. The colour in my interiors comes from curtains, pillows, carpets and art. **Best idea:** Working out the budget so that there is enough to spend on art... but my smartest move has been to work with NoOffice. Together we have created residential-like, highly unusual office spaces. **Big break:** I have been in business for nearly 20 years, but as a company - the partnership is one year old - the break was the NoOffice project in the Docklands and the subsequent office spaces that we are now designing. **Biggest influence:** I spend lots of money on interior magazines and books, because design is a reinvention process and you have to be aware of what other people are doing. **Motivation:** The pleasure of seeing design work. **New directions:** I always take traditional design fundamentals into each job, but combine them with new trends and put the whole scheme together in a different way on every project. **Favourite painting:** A painting in my dining room by Anne Sophie Blytt. It has great depth and is very modern.

The whole canvas is in a brownish taupe and has large black lines that appear to be like two rivers crossing... but equally it can look like something disappearing into the horizon. **Favourite movie star:** Jude Law - there is something intriguing about his face. He has the ability to change his appearance to suit every part he plays. **Favourite country:** France for the culture and the climate, and Britain for its people. **Free time:** Walking my English bulldog, Augusta, and travel and cooking. **Top shop:** Appley Hoare on Pimlico Road in London for its' complex and different mix of furniture and objects that creates a kind of French-English-Tuscan country look. **Pet hates:** Anything that matches.

'You don't necessarily have to spend the entire budget on furniture and textiles... I prefer to spend the money on art.'

Contents & Directory of Designers

4
Jean de Meulder
Koniklijkelaan 60
2600 Antwerp
Belgium
Tel : (32) 32 30 15 45
Fax : (32) 32 30 16 77

12
MM Design
The Studio
Redloh House
2 Michael Road
London SW6 2AD
Tel : (44 20) 7751 0171
Fax : (44 20) 7751 0172

18
Isobel Czarska
9-15 Neal Street
London WC2 9PW
Tel : (44 20) 7836 6991
Fax : (44 20) 7836 3979

22
Hennie Interiors
Bennechesgt 1
0169 Oslo
Norway
Tel : (47) 22 06 85 86
Fax : (47) 22 06 85 87

28
Ciao
43 Ebury Mews
London SW1W 9EA
Tel : (44 20) 7881 9840
Fax : (44 20) 7881 9841

36
Shiuli Johanna Interiors
14 Archery Steps
St. George's Fields
London W2 2YF
Tel : (44 20) 7724 4984
Fax : (44 20) 77246701

40
Jean-Pierre Heurteau
781 High Street
Armadale 3143
Victoria
Australia
Tel : (61) 3 9576 1349
Fax : (61) 3 9509 9920

44
Insight
45-125 Panorama Drive
Palm Desert
CA 92260
USA
Tel : (760) 568 9089
Fax : (760) 340 3822

52
First Editions
157 Cathedral Street
Woolloomooloo
NSW
Tel : (61) 293 802 122
Fax : (61) 293 802 677

54
Esboco Interiors
Rua Princesa Dona
Amelia 5
9000 Funchal
Madeira
Portugal
Tel : (351) 291 204 370
Fax: (351) 291 204 379

58
Terence Disdale Designs
31 The Green
Richmond
Surrey
TW9 1LX
Tel : (44 20) 8940 1452
Fax : (44 20) 8940 5964

66
Eren Yorulmazer
Abdi Igetkci Cad
382 Matca
Istanbul
Turkey
Tel : (90) 212 219 5774
Fax : (90) 212 219 7230

70
TMH
208 The Chambers
Chelsea Habour
London SW10 0XF
Tel : (44 20) 7349 9017
Fax : (44 20) 7349 9018

76
JBA Interiors
1930 Chestnut Street
Philadelphia
PA 19103
USA
Tel : (215) 557 6449
Fax : (215) 751 0734

80
Joseph Sy & Associates
17/F Heng Shan Centre
145 Queen's Road East
Wanchai
Hong Kong
Tel : (852) 2866 1333
Fax : (852) 2866 1222

82
Jorge A Lacarra
Via Natale del Grande 8
Trastevere
Roma 00153
Italy
Tel/Fax : (39) 06 588 3415

86
Lifestyles
48 Old Church Street
London SW3 5BY
Tel : (44 20) 7349 8020
Fax : (44 20) 7349 8021

90
Steve Leung
Room 2401 CC Wu Building
302 Hennessy Road
Wanchai
Hong Kong
Tel : (852 25) 27 1600
Fax : (852 25) 27 2071

96
David Carter
109 Mile End Road
Stepney Green
London E1 4UJ
Tel : (44 20) 7790 0259
Mobile : 07973 653944

104
ek Reedy Interiors Inc
PMB 25167
P.O. Box 20,000
Jackson WY 83001
Tel : (307) 739 9121
Fax : (307) 734 9079

110
Associates III Inc
1516 Blake Street
Denver
CO 80202
USA
Tel : (303) 534 4444
Fax : (303) 629 5035

116
Lannis Peta Spiro Interiors
2 Grace Avenue
Shenley
Herts
WD7 9DN
Tel : (44) 1923 855271
Fax : (44) 1923 850817

118
Alberto Pinto
Hotel de la Victoire 11
Rue d'Aboukir
75002 Paris
France
Tel : (33) 1 4013 75 87
Fax : (33) 1 4013 75 80

128
Sara A. Al Faisal
Alssamoure Design Associates
P.O. Box 15707
Riyadh
Saudi Arabia
Tel : (966) 1 4412723
Fax : (966) 1 4412651

134
Lantis-Bain Scorgie
P.O. box 411651
Craighall
2024 Gauteng
South Africa
Tel : (27) 11 448 2578
Fax : (27) 11 448 2522

140
Decollo
838 High Street
Armadale, Victoria
Australia
Tel : 03 9500 9422
Fax : 03 9576 0003

144
Emmanuel Gomes
Rua do Barao 18-B
1100-073 Lisbon
Portugal
Tel : (351) 21 886 5690
Fax : (351) 21 887 0005

150
Petra Schlapp
Feldstrasse 23
63303 Dreieich
Germany
Tel : (49) 171 3645043 (Europe)
Tel : 001 720 201 1999 (USA)

160
KSR Clifton
14 Greenland Street
London NW1 0ND
Tel : (44 20) 7 692 5000
(44 20) 7 586 5533
Fax : (44 20) 7 692 5050

164
Gluckstein Design
234 Davenport Road
Toronto
Ontario M5R 1J6
Tel : (416) 928 2067
Fax : (416) 928 2114

168
Azul Tierra
Angel Lozano 2
Alicante 03001
Spain
Tel : (34) 965 208340
Fax : (34) 965 140203

174
Hare & Klein
138 Cathedral Street
Woolloomooloo
NSW 2011
Australia
Tel : (61) 2 9368 1234
Fax : (61) 9368 1020

176
Jestico & Whiles
1 Cobourg Street
London NW1 2HP
Tel : (44 20) 7380 0382
Fax : (44 20) 7380 0511

182
Moe & lena
Erling Skjalgssonsgt 24
0267 Oslo
Norway
Tel : (47) 232 70623
Fax : (47) 232 70624